BY STEVE LEWIS

EASY INDIAN COOKING

36 Tasty Recipes

Chicken Tikka

Cooking times may vary depending on the size and thickness of the food

Chicken Tikka

Ingredients

- 500g boneless chicken, cut into large pieces
- 1 cup yogurt
- 1 tablespoon lemon juice
- 2 teaspoons ginger paste
- 2 teaspoons garlic paste
- 2 teaspoons paprika
- 1 teaspoon cumin
- 1 teaspoon coriander
- 1 teaspoon garam masala
- Salt, to taste
- 2 tablespoons oil

Instructions

- In a large bowl, mix the yogurt, lemon juice, ginger paste, garlic paste, paprika, cumin, coriander, garam masala, salt, and oil.
- Add the chicken pieces to the marinade and mix until well coated.
- Cover and refrigerate for at least 1 hour or overnight.
- Preheat the air fryer to 200°C.
- Arrange the chicken pieces in a single layer in the air fryer basket, making sure not to overcrowd.
- Cook for 15 minutes or until the chicken is cooked through and the skin is crispy and golden brown.
- Serve hot with your favorite dipping sauce.
- **Recommended cooking time: 15 minutes at 200°C**

Lamb Kofta

Cooking times may vary depending on the size and thickness of the food

Lamb Kofta

Ingredients

- 500g ground lamb
- 1 onion, finely chopped
- 2 cloves garlic, minced
- 1 teaspoon coriander
- 1 teaspoon cumin
- 1 teaspoon garam masala
- Salt, to taste
- 2 tablespoons oil

Instructions

- In a large bowl, mix the ground lamb, onion, garlic, coriander, cumin, garam masala, salt, and oil.
- Shape the mixture into oval-shaped balls about 3 cm in diameter.
- Preheat the air fryer to 200°C.
- Arrange the kofta in a single layer in the air fryer basket, making sure not to overcrowd.
- Cook for 12 minutes or until the kofta are browned and cooked
- through.
- Serve hot with your favorite dipping sauce.

Recommended cooking time: 12 minutes at 200°C

Pork Vindaloo

Cooking times may vary depending on the size and thickness of the food

Pork Vindaloo

Ingredients

- 500g boneless pork, cut into large pieces
- 1 onion, finely chopped
- 2 cloves garlic, minced
- 2 teaspoons ginger paste
- 2 teaspoons cumin
- 1 teaspoon coriander
- 1 teaspoon turmeric
- 1 teaspoon cayenne pepper
- 1 teaspoon paprika
- Salt, to taste
- 2 tablespoons oil

Instructions

- In a large bowl, mix the onion, garlic, ginger paste, cumin, coriander, turmeric, cayenne pepper, paprika, salt, and oil.
- Add the pork pieces to the mixture and mix until well coated.
- Preheat the air fryer to 200°C.
- Arrange the pork pieces in a single layer in the air fryer basket, making sure not to overcrowd.
- Cook for 20 minutes or until the pork is cooked through and the sauce has thickened.
- Serve hot with rice.
- **Recommended cooking time: 20 minutes at 200°C**

Fish Masala

Cooking times may vary depending on the size and thickness of the food

Fish Masala

Ingredients

- 500g firm white fish, cut into large pieces
- 1 onion, finely chopped
- 2 cloves garlic, minced
- 2 teaspoons ginger paste
- 2 teaspoons cumin
- 1 teaspoon coriander
- 1 teaspoon turmeric
- 1 teaspoon paprika
- Salt, to taste
- 2 tablespoons oil

Instructions

- In a large bowl, mix the onion, garlic, ginger paste, cumin, coriander, turmeric, paprika, salt, and oil.
- Add the fish pieces to the mixture and mix until well coated.
- Preheat the air fryer to 200°C.
- Arrange the fish pieces in a single layer in the air fryer basket, making sure not to overcrowd.
- Cook for 10 minutes or until the fish is cooked through and the skin is crispy and golden brown.
- Serve hot with lemon wedges and a side of rice.
- **Recommended cooking time: 10 minutes at 200°C**

Beef Korma

Cooking times may vary depending on the size and thickness of the food

Beef Korma

Ingredients

- 500g beef, cut into large pieces
- 1 onion, finely chopped
- 2 cloves garlic, minced
- 2 teaspoons ginger paste
- 1 cup yogurt
- 2 teaspoons coriander
- 1 teaspoon cumin
- 1 teaspoon garam masala
- Salt, to taste
- 2 tablespoons oil

Instructions

- In a large bowl, mix the onion, garlic, ginger paste, yogurt, coriander, cumin, garam masala, salt, and oil.
- Add the beef pieces to the mixture and mix until well coated.
- Cover and refrigerate for at least 1 hour or overnight.
- Preheat the air fryer to 200°C.
- Arrange the beef pieces in a single layer in the air fryer basket, making sure not to overcrowd.
- Cook for 18 minutes or until the beef is cooked through and the sauce has thickened.
- Serve hot with rice.
- **Recommended cooking time: 18 minutes at 200°C**

Chicken Biryani

Cooking times may vary depending on the size and thickness of the food

Chicken Biryani

Ingredients

- 500g boneless chicken, cut into large pieces
- 1 cup basmati rice
- 1 onion, finely chopped
- 2 cloves garlic, minced
- 2 teaspoons ginger paste
- 2 teaspoons cumin
- 1 teaspoon coriander
- 1 teaspoon turmeric
- 1 teaspoon paprika
- Salt, to taste
- 2 tablespoons oil

Instructions

- In a large bowl, mix the onion, garlic, ginger paste, cumin, coriander, turmeric, paprika, salt, and oil.
- Add the chicken pieces to the mixture and mix until well coated.
- Rinse the rice and place it in a large saucepan with 2 cups of water. Bring to a boil, then reduce the heat and simmer for 10 minutes or until the water is absorbed and the rice is tender.
- Preheat the air fryer to 200°C.
- Spread half of the rice in the bottom of the air fryer basket. Arrange the chicken pieces on top of the rice and cover with the remaining rice.
- Cook for 20 minutes or until the chicken is cooked through and the rice is fluffy and aromatic.
- Serve hot with raita or chutney.
- **Recommended cooking time: 20 minutes at 200°C**

Vegetable Samosas

Cooking times may vary depending on the size and thickness of the food

Vegetable Samosas

Ingredients

- 500g frozen samosas
- 2 tablespoons oil

Instructions

- Preheat the air fryer to 200°C.
- Brush the samosas with oil on all sides.
- Arrange the samosas in a single layer in the air fryer basket, making sure not to overcrowd.
- Cook for 10-12 minutes or until the samosas are crispy and golden brown.
- Serve hot with chutney or ketchup.
- **Recommended cooking time: 10-12 minutes at 200°C**

Lamb Chops

Cooking times may vary depending on the size and thickness of the food

Lamb Chops

Ingredients

- 8 lamb chops
- 1 teaspoon cumin
- 1 teaspoon coriander
- 1 teaspoon paprika
- Salt, to taste
- 2 tablespoons oil

Instructions

- In a large bowl, mix the cumin, coriander, paprika, salt, and oil.
- Add the lamb chops to the mixture and mix until well coated.
- Preheat the air fryer to 200°C.
- Arrange the lamb chops in a single layer in the air fryer basket making sure not to overcrowd.
- Cook for 12 minutes or until the lamb chops are cooked through and the spices are aromatic.
- Serve hot with a side of vegetables or rice.
- **Recommended cooking time: 12 minutes at 200°C**

Pork Ribs

Cooking times may vary depending on the size and thickness of the food

Pork Ribs

Ingredients

- 1kg pork ribs
- 2 tablespoons BBQ sauce
- 2 tablespoons honey
- Salt, to taste

Instructions

- In a large bowl, mix the BBQ sauce, honey, and salt.
- Add the pork ribs to the mixture and mix until well coated.
- Preheat the air fryer to 200°C.
- Arrange the pork ribs in a single layer in the air fryer basket, making sure not to overcrowd.
- Cook for 20 minutes or until the pork ribs are cooked through and the sauce is sticky and caramelized
- Serve hot with a side of vegetables or rice.
- **Recommended cooking time: 20 minutes at 200°C**

Vegetable Pakoras

Cooking times may vary depending on the size and thickness of the food

Vegetable Pakoras

Ingredients

- 2 cups mixed vegetables
  (such as onion, capsicum, eggplant, and potato),
  chopped into bite-sized pieces
- 1 cup besan (chickpea flour)
- 1 teaspoon cumin
- 1 teaspoon coriander
- 1 teaspoon paprika
- Salt, to taste
- Water, as needed

Instructions

- In a large bowl, mix the besan, cumin, coriander, paprika, salt, and enough water to form a batter.
- Add the vegetables to the mixture and mix until well coated.
- Preheat the air fryer to 200°C.
- Using a spoon, drop spoonfuls of the batter into the air fryer basket making sure not to overcrowd.
- Cook for 10 minutes or until the pakoras are crispy and golden brown.
- Serve hot with chutney or ketchup.
- **Recommended cooking time: 10 minutes at 200°C**

Tandoori Chicken

Cooking times may vary depending on the size and thickness of the food

Tandoori Chicken

Ingredients

- 1 kg chicken pieces (thighs, drumsticks, or breast)
- 1 cup plain yogurt
- 2 tablespoons tandoori masala
- 2 tablespoons lemon juice
- Salt, to taste
- 2 tablespoons oil

Instructions

- In a large bowl, mix the yogurt, tandoori masala, lemon juice, salt, and oil.
- Add the chicken pieces to the mixture and mix until well coated.
- Cover and marinate the chicken for at least 2 hours or overnight in the refrigerator.
- Preheat the air fryer to 200°C.
- Arrange the chicken pieces in a single layer in the air fryer basket, making sure not to overcrowd.
- Cook for 20 minutes or until the chicken is cooked through and the skin is golden brown and crispy.
- Serve hot with a side of rice and vegetables.
- **Recommended cooking time: 20 minutes at 200°C**

Aloo Tikki

Cooking times may vary depending on the size and thickness of the food

Aloo Tikki

Ingredients

- 2 large potatoes, peeled and grated
- 1 onion, finely chopped
- 2 tablespoons besan (chickpea flour)
- 1 teaspoon cumin
- 1 teaspoon coriander
- Salt, to taste
- 2 tablespoons oil

Instructions

- In a large bowl, mix the grated potatoes, onion, besan, cumin, coriander, salt, and oil.
- Shape the mixture into small patties.
- Preheat the air fryer to 200°C.
- Place the patties in the air fryer basket, making sure not to overcrowd.
- Cook for 10 minutes on each side or until the tikkis are crispy and golden brown.
- Serve hot with chutney or ketchup
- **Recommended cooking time: 10 minutes on each side at 200°C**

Butter Chicken

Cooking times may vary depending on the size and thickness of the food

Butter Chicken

Ingredients

- 1 kg chicken pieces (thighs, drumsticks, or breast)
- 2 tablespoons butter
- 1 onion, finely chopped
- 4 cloves garlic, minced
- 2 tablespoons tomato paste
- 1 cup tomato puree
- 1 tablespoon garam masala
- 1 tablespoon kasoori methi (dried fenugreek leaves)
- Salt, to taste
- 1 cup heavy cream
- 2 tablespoons fresh cilantro, chopped

Instructions

- Preheat the air fryer to 200°C.
- Arrange the chicken pieces in a single layer in the air fryer basket, making sure not to overcrowd.
- Cook for 15 minutes or until the chicken is cooked through and the skin is golden brown and crispy.
- In a separate pan, melt the butter over medium heat.
- Add the onion and garlic and cook until softened.
- Add the tomato paste, tomato puree, garam masala, kasoori methi, salt, and heavy cream.
- Stir to combine and simmer for 10 minutes or until the sauce has thickened.
- Add the cooked chicken to the sauce and stir to coat.
- Serve hot with rice and a sprinkle of fresh cilantro.
- **Recommended cooking time: 15 minutes at 200°C**

Masoor Dal

Cooking times may vary depending on the size and thickness of the food

Masoor Dal

Ingredients

- 1 cup masoor dal (red lentils)
- 2 teaspoons turmeric
- 2 tablespoons ghee
- 1 teaspoon cumin
- 1 teaspoon coriander
- Salt, to taste
- 2 tablespoons fresh cilantro, chopped

Instructions

- Rinse the masoor dal in a colander and set aside.
- In a large pot, heat the ghee over medium heat.
- Add the cumin and coriander and cook until fragrant.
- Add the masoor dal, turmeric, salt, and 4 cups of water.
- Stir to combine and bring to a boil.
- Reduce heat to low and simmer for 20 minutes or until the dal is soft and has broken down.
- Use a hand blender to puree the dal until smooth.
- **Stir in the fresh cilantro and serve hot with rice and naan.**

Fish Curry

Cooking times may vary depending on the size and thickness of the food

Fish Curry

Ingredients

- 1 kg fish fillets (tilapia or cod)
- 2 tablespoons oil
- 1 onion, finely chopped
- 2 cloves garlic, minced
- 2 tablespoons ginger, grated
- 2 tablespoons tomato paste
- 1 cup coconut milk
- 1 teaspoon coriander
- 1 teaspoon cumin
- Salt, to taste
- 2 tablespoons fresh cilantro, chopped

Instructions

- In a large pan, heat the oil over medium heat.
- Add the onion, garlic, and ginger and cook until softened.
- Add the tomato paste, coconut milk, coriander, cumin, salt, and 1 cup of water.
- Stir to combine and bring to a boil.
- Reduce heat to low and simmer for 10 minutes or until the sauce has thickened.
- Preheat the air fryer to 200°C.
- Arrange the fish fillets in a single layer in the air fryer basket, making sure not to overcrowd.
- Cook for 10 minutes or until the fish is cooked through and flaky.
- Serve hot with rice and the sauce spooned over the top.
- **Recommended cooking time: 10 minutes at 200°C**

Beef Biryani

Cooking times may vary depending on the size and thickness of the food

Beef Biryani

Ingredients

- 500 g beef, cut into bite-sized pieces
- 1 onion, finely chopped
- 2 tablespoons ginger, grated
- 2 cloves garlic, minced
- 2 tablespoons tomato paste
- 1 teaspoon coriander
- 1 teaspoon cumin
- 1 teaspoon turmeric
- Salt, to taste
- 2 cups basmati rice
- 4 cups chicken broth
- 2 tablespoons oil
- 2 tablespoons fresh cilantro, chopped

Instructions

- In a large pan, heat the oil over medium heat.
- Add the onion, ginger, and garlic and cook until softened.
- Add the beef and cook until browned on all sides.
- Add the tomato paste, coriander, cumin, turmeric, salt, and chicken broth.
- Stir to combine and bring to a boil.
- Reduce heat to low and simmer for 15 minutes or until the beef is tender.
- In a separate pot, cook the basmati rice according to package instructions.
- Preheat the air fryer to 200°C.
- In a large bowl, mix the cooked rice and beef mixture together.
- Place the biryani in the air fryer basket, making sure not to overcrowd.
- Cook for 10 minutes or until heated through.
- Serve hot with a sprinkle of fresh cilantro.
- **Recommended cooking time: 10 minutes at 200°C**

Lamb Rogan Josh

Cooking times may vary depending on the size and thickness of the food

Lamb Rogan Josh

Ingredients

- 500 g lamb, cut into bite-sized pieces
- 2 tablespoons oil
- 1 onion, finely chopped
- 2 cloves garlic, minced
- 2 tablespoons ginger, grated
- 2 tablespoons tomato paste
- 1 teaspoon coriander
- 1 teaspoon cumin
- 1 teaspoon turmeric
- Salt, to taste
- 1 cup chicken broth
- 2 tablespoons fresh cilantro, chopped

Instructions

- In a large pan, heat the oil over medium heat.
- Add the onion, garlic, and ginger and cook until softened.
- Add the lamb and cook until browned on all sides.
- Add the tomato paste, coriander, cumin, turmeric, salt, and chicken broth.
- Stir to combine and bring to a boil.
- Reduce heat to low and simmer for 20 minutes or until the lamb is tender.
- Preheat the air fryer to 200°C.
- Arrange the lamb pieces in a single layer in the air fryer basket, making sure not to overcrowd.
- Cook for 10 minutes or until heated through.
- Serve hot with a sprinkle of fresh cilantro.
- **Recommended cooking time: 10 minutes at 200°C**

Chicken Korma

Cooking times may vary depending on the size and thickness of the food

Chicken Korma

Ingredients

- 500g chicken, cut into bite-sized pieces
- 2 tablespoons oil
- 1 onion, finely chopped
- 2 cloves garlic, minced
- 2 tablespoons ginger, grated
- 2 tablespoons tomato paste
- 1 teaspoon coriander
- 1 teaspoon cumin
- 1 teaspoon turmeric
- Salt, to taste
- 1 cup chicken broth
- 1 cup plain yogurt
- 2 tablespoons fresh cilantro, chopped

Instructions

- In a large pan, heat the oil over medium heat.
- Add the onion, garlic, and ginger and cook until softened.
- Add the chicken and cook until browned on all sides.
- Add the tomato paste, coriander, cumin, turmeric, salt, chicken broth, and yogurt.
- Stir to combine and bring to a boil.
- Reduce heat to low and simmer for 20 minutes or until the chicken is cooked through.
- Preheat the air fryer to 200°C.
- Arrange the chicken pieces in a single layer in the air fryer basket, making sure not to overcrowd.
- Cook for 10 minutes or until heated through.
- Serve hot with a sprinkle of fresh cilantro.
- **Recommended cooking time: 10 minutes at 200°C**

Tandoori Chicken Wings

Cooking times may vary depending on the size and thickness of the food

Tandoori Chicken Wings

Ingredients

- 500 g chicken wings
- 1 cup plain yogurt
- 2 tablespoons lemon juice
- 1 tablespoon garam masala
- 1 tablespoon chili powder
- 1 tablespoon cumin
- 1 tablespoon coriander
- Salt, to taste

Instructions

- In a large bowl, mix together the yogurt, lemon juice, garam masala, chili powder, cumin, coriander, and salt.
- Add the chicken wings to the bowl and mix until well coated.
- Cover and refrigerate for at least 2 hours, or overnight.
- Preheat the air fryer to 200°C.
- Arrange the chicken wings in a single layer in the air fryer basket, making sure not to overcrowd.
- Cook for 20 minutes or until crispy and golden brown.
- Serve hot with a dollop of raita and lemon wedges.
- **Recommended cooking time: 20 minutes at 200°C**

Fish Tikka Masala

Cooking times may vary depending on the size and thickness of the food

Fish Tikka Masala

Ingredients

- 500 g fish fillets
- 1 cup plain yogurt
- 2 tablespoons lemon juice
- 1 tablespoon garam masala
- 1 tablespoon chili powder
- 1 tablespoon coriander
- Salt, to taste

Instructions

- In a large bowl, mix together the yogurt, lemon juice, garam masala, chili powder, coriander, and salt.
- Add the fish fillets to the bowl and mix until well coated.
- Cover and refrigerate for at least 2 hours, or overnight.
- Preheat the air fryer to 200°C.
- Arrange the fish fillets in a single layer in the air fryer basket, making sure not to overcrowd.
- Cook for 10 minutes or until cooked through and flaky.
- Serve hot with steamed rice and a side of chutney.
- **Recommended cooking time: 10 minutes at 200°C**

Lamb Kofta Kebabs

Cooking times may vary depending on the size and thickness of the food

Lamb Kofta Kebabs

Ingredients

- 500g ground lamb
- 1 onion, grated
- 2 cloves garlic, minced
- 2 tablespoons ginger, grated
- 2 tablespoons fresh cilantro, chopped
- 2 tablespoons breadcrumbs
- 1 teaspoon cumin
- 1 teaspoon coriander
- 1 teaspoon paprika
- Salt, to taste
- Skewers

Instructions

- In a large bowl, mix together the ground lamb, onion, garlic, ginger, cilantro, breadcrumbs, cumin, coriander, paprika, and salt.
- Shape the mixture into balls around the skewers.
- Preheat the air fryer to 200°C.
- Arrange the kofta kebabs in a single layer in the air fryer basket, making sure not to overcrowd.
- Cook for 15 minutes or until crispy and golden brown.
- Serve hot with a side of rice, naan, and chutney.
- **Recommended cooking time: 15 minutes at 200°C**

Beef Seekh Kebabs

Cooking times may vary depending on the size and thickness of the food

Beef Seekh Kebabs

Ingredients

- 500 g ground beef
- 1 onion, grated
- 2 cloves garlic, minced
- 2 tablespoons ginger, grated
- 2 tablespoons fresh mint, chopped
- 2 tablespoons breadcrumbs
- 1 teaspoon cumin
- 1 teaspoon coriander
- 1 teaspoon paprika
- Salt, to taste
- Skewers

Instructions

- In a large bowl, mix together the ground beef, onion, garlic, ginger, mint, breadcrumbs, cumin, coriander, paprika, and salt.
- Shape the mixture into sausage shapes around the skewers.
- Preheat the air fryer to 200°C.
- Arrange the seekh kebabs in a single layer in the air fryer basket, making sure not to overcrowd.
- Cook for 15 minutes or until crispy and golden brown.
- Serve hot with a side of rice, naan, and chutney.
- **Recommended cooking time: 15 minutes at 200°C**

Shrimp Biryani

Cooking times may vary depending on the size and thickness of the food

Shrimp Biryani

Ingredients

- 500g large shrimp, peeled and deveined
- 2 cups basmati rice
- 2 onions, sliced
- 2 cloves garlic, minced
- 2 tablespoons ginger, grated
- 2 tomatoes, chopped
- 1 cup frozen peas
- 2 tablespoons biryani masala
- Salt, to taste
- 2 tablespoons oil
- 2 cups chicken stock

Instructions

- In a large pan, heat the oil over medium heat.
- Add the onions, garlic, and ginger and cook until softened.
- Add the shrimp and cook until pink and slightly charred.
- Add the tomatoes, peas, biryani masala, and salt.
- Stir to combine and bring to a boil.
- Reduce heat to low and simmer for 10 minutes or until the shrimp is cooked through.
- In a separate pan, cook the rice in boiling water for 10 minutes or until tender.
- Preheat the air fryer to 200°C.
- In a large bowl, mix together the shrimp mixture and rice.
- Transfer the mixture to the air fryer basket and spread out evenly.
- Cook for 10 minutes or until heated through.
- Serve hot with a dollop of raita and lemon wedges.
- **Recommended cooking time: 10 minutes at 200°C**

Spicy Chicken Wings with Mint Yogurt Dip

Cooking times may vary depending on the size and thickness of the food

Spicy Chicken Wings with Mint Yogurt Dip

Ingredients

- 1 kilogram chicken wings
- 2 tablespoons chili powder
- 1 tablespoon cumin
- 1 tablespoon coriander
- 1 teaspoon turmeric
- 1 teaspoon garam masala
- Salt, to taste
- 1 tablespoon oil

For the dip:

- 1 cup plain yogurt
- 1/2 cup mint leaves, chopped
- 1 clove garlic, minced
- Salt, to taste

Instructions

- In a large pan, heat the oil over medium heat.
- In a large bowl, combine the chicken wings, chili powder, cumin, coriander, turmeric, garam masala, salt, and oil.
- Mix well to coat the chicken.
- Preheat the air fryer to 200°C.
- Place the chicken wings in a single layer in the air fryer basket.
- Cook for 20-25 minutes or until crispy and golden brown.
- While the chicken is cooking, mix together the yogurt, mint, garlic, and salt for the dip.
- Serve the spicy chicken wings with the mint yogurt dip.
- **Recommended cooking time: 20-25 minutes at 200°C**

Lamb Chops with Cilantro Chutney

Cooking times may vary depending on the size and thickness of the food

Lamb Chops with Cilantro Chutney

Ingredients

- 4 lamb chops
- 2 tablespoons cumin
- 2 tablespoons coriander
- 2 tablespoons turmeric
- Salt, to taste
- 2 tablespoons oil

For the chutney:

- 2 cups cilantro leaves
- 1 cup mint leaves
- 2 green chili peppers
- 2 cloves garlic
- Salt, to taste
- 1/2 cup water

Instructions

- In a large bowl, combine the lamb chops, cumin, coriander, turmeric, salt, and oil. Mix well to coat the lamb.
- Preheat the air fryer to 200°C.
- Place the lamb chops in a single layer in the air fryer basket.
- Cook for 10-15 minutes or until cooked to your desired doneness.
- While the lamb is cooking, make the chutney by blending together the cilantro, mint, green chili peppers, garlic, salt, and water.
- Serve the lamb chops with the cilantro chutney.
- **Recommended cooking time: 10-15 minutes at 200°C**

Pork Belly with Five-Spice Powder

Cooking times may vary depending on the size and thickness of the food

Pork Belly with Five-Spice Powder

Ingredients

- 500 grams pork belly
- 2 tablespoons five-spice powder
- Salt, to taste
- 2 tablespoons oil

Instructions

- In a large bowl, combine the pork belly, five-spice powder, salt, and oil.
- Mix well to coat the pork.
- Preheat the air fryer to 200°C.
- Place the pork belly in a single layer in the air fryer basket.
- Cook for 20-25 minutes or until crispy and golden brown.
- Serve hot, garnished with chopped scallions if desired.
- **Recommended cooking time: 20-25 minutes at 200°C**

Air-Fried Beef Keema

Cooking times may vary depending on the size and thickness of the food

Air-Fried Beef Keema

Ingredients

- 500g beef mince
- 1 onion, chopped
- 2 garlic cloves, minced
- 1 tsp ginger paste
- 1 tsp cumin powder
- 1 tsp coriander powder
- 1 tsp garam masala
- 1 tsp turmeric
- Salt to taste
- **Cooking time: 15-20 minutes at 200°C**

Instructions

- In a pan, heat some oil and sauté the onion until softened.
- Add the garlic and ginger paste and cook for another minute.
- Add the beef mince and cook until browned.
  Add the cumin powder, coriander powder, garam masala,
- turmeric and salt. Mix well.
- Spoon the mixture into the air fryer basket
  and cook at 200°C for 15-20 minutes or until fully cooked.
- Serve with roti or rice.
  Cooking time: 15-20 minutes at 200°C

Masala Fried Fish

Cooking times may vary depending on the size and thickness of the food

Masala Fried Fish

Ingredients

- 4 fish fillets
- 1 cup all-purpose flour
- 1 tsp. red chili powder
- 1 tsp. turmeric powder
- 1 tsp. coriander powder
- 1 tsp. cumin powder
- Salt to taste
- Oil for brushing

Instructions

- In a mixing bowl, combine the flour, red chili powder, turmeric powder, coriander powder, cumin powder, and salt.
- Dip the fish fillets in the flour mixture, making sure they are well coated.
- Preheat the air fryer to 200°C for 3 minutes.
- Place the coated fish fillets in the air fryer basket and brush with oil.
- Cook for 10-12 minutes, until crispy and fully cooked.
- Serve hot with lemon wedges and mint chutney.
- **Cooking Time: 10-12 minutes**

Air-Fried Paneer Tikka

Cooking times may vary depending on the size and thickness of the food

Air-Fried Paneer Tikka

Ingredients

- 200g paneer, cut into 1-inch cubes
- 1 cup plain yoghurt
- 1 tsp ginger paste
- 1 tsp garlic paste
- 1 tsp turmeric powder
- 1 tsp cumin powder
- 1 tsp coriander powder
- Salt to taste
- 1 tbsp lemon juice
- 1 tbsp oil
- Skewers (optional)

Instructions

- In a large bowl, mix together the paneer cubes, yoghurt, ginger paste, garlic paste, turmeric powder, cumin powder, coriander powder, salt, lemon juice, and oil.
- Marinate the paneer cubes for 30 minutes to 1 hour.
- If using skewers, thread the marinated paneer cubes onto the skewers.
- Place the skewers (or paneer cubes if not using skewers) in the air fryer basket and cook at 200°C for 8-10 minutes, until they are golden brown and slightly charred on both sides.
- Serve the Air-Fried Paneer Tikka with your favourite chutney or sauce.
- **Cooking Time: 8-10 minutes at 200°C.**

Air-Fried Baingan Bharta

Cooking times may vary depending on the size and thickness of the food

Air-Fried Baingan Bharta

Ingredients

- 2 medium eggplants
- 1 tbsp oil
- 1 medium onion, finely chopped
- 2 medium tomatoes, finely chopped
- 1 tsp ginger paste
- 1 tsp garlic paste
- 1 tsp cumin powder
- 1 tsp coriander powder
- 1 tsp turmeric powder
- Salt to taste
- 1/4 cup chopped coriander leaves

Instructions

- Prick the eggplants with a fork and place them in the air fryer basket.
- Cook at 200°C for 15-20 minutes, until they are charred and soft.
- Once the eggplants are cool enough to handle, peel off the skin and mash the flesh.
- In a pan, heat the oil and sauté the onion until golden brown.
- Add the ginger paste, garlic paste, cumin powder, coriander powder, turmeric powder, and salt, and cook for 2-3 minutes.
- Add the chopped tomatoes and cook until they are soft and pulpy.
- Stir in the mashed eggplant and cook for another 2-3 minutes. Garnish with chopped coriander leaves and serve the Air-Fried
- Baingan Bharta with roti or rice.

Cooking Time: 15-20 minutes at 200°C for the eggplants, and 10-15 minutes on the stovetop for the bharta.

Air-Fried Masala Okra

Cooking times may vary depending on the size and thickness of the food

Air-Fried Masala Okra

Ingredients

- 500g okra
- 2 tbsp oil
- 2 tsp cumin seeds
- 1 tsp mustard seeds
- 2 tbsp coriander powder
- 1 tsp garam masala
- 1 tsp red chilli powder
- 1 tsp turmeric
- Salt to taste

Instructions

- Wash and dry the okra. Cut off the tops and tails.
- In a bowl, mix together 2 tbsp oil with 2 tsp cumin seeds,
- 1 tsp mustard seeds, 2 tbsp coriander powder,
- 1 tsp garam masala, 1 tsp red chilli powder, 1 tsp turmeric, and salt to taste.
- Add the okra to the bowl and mix well to coat each piece.
- Preheat the air fryer to 200°C for 3 minutes.
- Arrange the okra in a single layer in the basket, making sure they do not touch each other.
- Air-fry for 10-12 minutes, or until crispy and browned.
- **Serve hot with rice or roti.**

Tandoori Chicken Thighs

Cooking times may vary depending on the size and thickness of the food

Tandoori Chicken Thighs

Ingredients

- 4 boneless chicken thighs
- 1 teaspoon turmeric
- 1 teaspoon paprika
- 1 teaspoon coriander
- 1 teaspoon cumin
- 1 teaspoon garam masala
- 1 teaspoon salt
- 1 teaspoon red chili powder
- 1 teaspoon garlic powder
- 1 teaspoon ginger powder
- 1 tablespoon lemon juice
- 2 tablespoons plain yogurt
- Cooking time: 20-25 minutes at 180°C

Instructions

- In a large mixing bowl, combine the turmeric, paprika, coriander,
- cumin, garam masala, salt, red chili powder, garlic powder,
- ginger powder, lemon juice, and yogurt.
- Mix well.
- Add the chicken to the bowl and mix until the chicken is coated evenly.
- Place the chicken in the air fryer basket, making sure not to overcrowd it.
- Cook at 180°C for 20-25 minutes, or until the internal temperature of the chicken reaches 165°F.
- Serve with rice and mint chutney.

Lamb Vindaloo

Cooking times may vary depending on the size and thickness of the food

Lamb Vindaloo

Ingredients

- 500g lamb, cut into bite-sized pieces
- 2 medium onions, diced
- 3 cloves garlic, minced
- 1 tablespoon ginger, minced
- 2 tablespoons tomato paste
- 2 tablespoons red wine vinegar
- 2 tablespoons garam masala
- 1 tablespoon turmeric
- 1 tablespoon paprika
- 1 tablespoon cumin
- 1 tablespoon coriander
- 1 tablespoon red chili powder
- 1 teaspoon salt
- 1 cup water
- **Cooking time: 20-25 minutes at 200°C**

Instructions

- In a large mixing bowl, combine the diced onions, minced garlic, minced ginger, tomato paste, red wine vinegar, garam masala, turmeric, paprika, cumin, coriander, red chili powder, and salt.
- Mix well.
- Add the lamb to the bowl and mix until the lamb is coated evenly.
- Place the lamb in the air fryer basket, making sure not to overcrowd it.
- Cook at 200°C for 20-25 minutes, or until the internal temperature of the lamb reaches 65°C.
- **Serve with rice and naan bread.**

Tandoori Chicken Curry

Cooking times may vary depending on the size and thickness of the food

Tandoori Chicken Curry

Ingredients

- 4 boneless chicken breasts
- 1 cup plain yogurt
- 1 tbsp lemon juice
- 2 tsp ginger paste
- 2 tsp garlic paste
- 2 tsp red chili powder
- 1 tsp cumin powder
- 1 tsp coriander powder
- 1 tsp garam masala
- 1 tsp turmeric powder
- Salt, to taste
- 1 onion, chopped
- 2 tomatoes, chopped
- 1 green chili, chopped
- 2 tsp oil

Instructions

- In a bowl, mix together the yogurt, lemon juice, ginger paste, garlic paste, red chili powder, cumin powder, coriander powder, garam masala, turmeric powder, and salt.
- Add the chicken breasts to the bowl and coat them evenly with the marinade.
- Cover the bowl and let it sit in the refrigerator for at least 30 minutes.
- Preheat the air fryer to 200°C.
- Place the chicken breasts in the air fryer basket and cook for 15-20 minutes or until they are fully cooked.
- In a pan, heat the oil over medium heat.
- Add the onion and green chili and sauté until the onion is translucent.
- Add the chopped tomatoes and cook until they are soft.
- Add the cooked chicken to the pan and simmer for 5-10 minutes or until the sauce thickens.
- Serve hot with rice or roti.

Paneer Tikka Masala

Cooking times may vary depending on the size and thickness of the food

Paneer Tikka Masala

Ingredients

- 300g paneer, cut into cubes
- 1 cup plain yogurt
- 1 tbsp lemon juice
- 2 tsp ginger paste
- 2 tsp garlic paste
- 2 tsp red chili powder
- 1 tsp cumin powder
- 1 tsp coriander powder
- 1 tsp garam masala
- 1 tsp turmeric powder
- Salt, to taste
- 1 onion, chopped
- 2 tomatoes, chopped
- 1 green chili, chopped
- 2 tsp oil
- 1 tsp cream

Instructions

- In a bowl, mix together the yogurt, lemon juice, ginger paste, garlic paste, red chili powder, cumin powder, coriander powder, garam masala, turmeric powder, and salt.
- Add the paneer cubes to the bowl and coat them evenly with the marinade.
- Cover the bowl and let it sit in the refrigerator for at least 30 minutes.
- Preheat the air fryer to 200°C.
- Place the paneer cubes in the air fryer basket and cook for 8-10 minutes or until they are slightly browned.
- In a pan, heat the oil over medium heat.
- Add the onion and green chili and sauté until the onion is translucent.
- Add the chopped tomatoes and cook until they are soft.
- Add the cooked paneer to the pan and simmer for 5-10 minutes or until the sauce thickens.
- Stir in the cream and simmer for another minute.
- **Serve hot with rice or roti.**

Aloo Gobi Masala

Cooking times may vary depending on the size and thickness of the food

Aloo Gobi Masala

Ingredients

- 2 large potatoes, peeled and diced
- 1 large head of cauliflower, chopped into florets
- 2 onions, chopped
- 2 tomatoes, chopped
- 2 tsp oil
- 1 tsp cumin powder
- 1 tsp coriander powder
- 1 tsp garam masala
- 1 tsp red chili powder
- 1 tsp turmeric powder
- Salt, to taste

Instructions

- Preheat the air fryer to 200°C.
- Place the diced potatoes in the air fryer basket and cook for 10-12 minutes or until they are soft.
- Place the chopped cauliflower in the air fryer basket and cook for 8-10 minutes or until it is slightly browned.
- In a pan, heat the oil over medium heat.
- Add the chopped onions and sauté until they are golden brown.
- Add the chopped tomatoes and cook until they are soft.
- Stir in the cumin powder, coriander powder, garam masala, red chili powder, and turmeric powder.
- Add the cooked potatoes and cauliflower to the pan and mix well.
- Season with salt to taste.
- Simmer for 5-10 minutes or until the sauce has thickened.
- **Serve hot with rice or roti.**

Printed in Great Britain
by Amazon